EXCLUSIONS

RECENT AND SELECTED TITLES FROM TUPELO PRESS

See our complete list at tupelopress.org

EXCLUSIONS

NOAH FALCK

T|P

TUPELO PRESS
North Adams, Massachesetts

Library of Congress Catalog-in-Publication data available upon request.
ISBN-13: 978-1-946482-33-4

Cover image: "Creative Commando number 3", Digital collage, 14" x 11", by Blick.
Copyright 2009. Used with permission.
Cover and text design by Howard Klein.

First paperback edition August 2020

Tupelo Press
P.O. Box 1767
North Adams, Massachusetts 01247
(413) 664-9611 / Fax: (413) 664-9711
editor@tupelopress.org / www.tupelopress.org

Tupelo Press is an award-winning independent literary press that publishes fine fiction, non-fiction, and poetry in books that are a joy to hold as well as read. Tupelo Press is a registered 501(c)(3) non-profit organization, and we rely on public support to carry out our mission of publishing extraordinary work that may be outside the realm of the large commercial publishers. Financial donations are welcome and are tax deductible.

for Sherri & Roza
and for everyone in the Rust Belt

I thought that if I could put it all down, that would be
one way. And next the thought came to me that to leave
all out would be another, and truer, way.

—*John Ashbery*

CONTENTS

POEM EXCLUDING FICTION

We live in the most fortunate of times.
And who's to blame. Our moods like
the four seasons in a tinted window
overlooking a bank robbery. Everyone
is raising children on cable television,
on leashes, on the slot machines that
have become our elegies. We live
other lives in high school, college, on
the porch reading the obituaries. Say *I
miss you* into the mirror while shaving,
brushing teeth, plucking something
that's meant to grow forever.

POEM EXCLUDING WAR

In those days it rained
until countries surrendered.
And then for more
than a moment there was no war.
Soldiers held hands
around a campfire
and over time began to blush.
Began to rename their machine
guns after flowers. Say something
you want to be remembered for.
Say the part no one
recognizes as song.

POEM EXCLUDING PUBLIC TRANSPORTATION

Like feral cats, the clouds drift and die
alone. And it just so happens that the
only road out of town wears a sunset
as a momentary god. And here is a
wind we title *Sober Cadence*. Stare down
until there is only argyle, until the
flowers have become targets in the
next world war. It's like breathing
through a straw in the future or
kissing a blind person in the middle of
an ocean. Give it a couple of minutes.

POEM EXCLUDING PASTORAL

You smoked and smoked
and smoked until the city
was a suburb occupied
by couples with hyphenated
last names, until your lungs
took the shape of tiny chimneys
in a cavern we couldn't mention
in everyday conversation without
some sort of secret handshake.

POEM EXCLUDING BIRTHDAY

If somewhere had a voice
it would come to us like fog.
Yellow fog over a street of gauze.
It would feel like the time you took
off your shirt and used it as a flag.
A flag in the blackout capital
of the world. Every memory
you have holding your breath
underwater in the deep end
with an erection. Or when you
called my body a surrealist's
dream with a kickstand.
At a certain age,
the mind digs for China
and like cold sores
the weather surrenders.

POEM EXCLUDING PARKING METERS

We index our love
on a street corner
crowded with a seething
arrangement of people
in mall wear. Your face
is October in another city
that's lost its mojo where
night comes down like a right fielder
in foul territory during post league
play. Teenagers can't get drunk fast
enough is what you think of
when you think of home.

POEM EXCLUDING FUTURE

Now the snow is black and we feel
dirty in its presence. Cigarette butts
blow across the wet pavement like
children leaving school during a bomb
threat. There's a good chance we have
no chance is what your thoughts are
during your daily commute to the
office. Roads break apart as variations
of sadness. And now the sky is all
truffles and shoe polish. It rehearses
the end over a cemetery full of
children trapped in moonlight.

POEM EXCLUDING THE METRIC SYSTEM

We take each other in like
secular holidays. Like
mountains through binoculars
in a televised storm. Here you
are, a shit show of everything
you've read online. And
there's such a revolutionary
clumsiness in the way you kiss
me goodbye through all of
August. The way you navigate
the workweek with something
like a cold war settling
on your eyelashes.

POEM EXCLUDING RELIGION

And on the seventh day
we wandered into obesity.
You wouldn't stop bleeding
soda pop from a paper cut
on your index finger.
A toothless man gave us a city
map made entirely of Milk Duds.
Our stomachs hummed
with what could only be
described as a *Sleepy Congress*.
Vultures circled us as if we were
already decomposing.
And we were.

POEM EXCLUDING CANCER

In graveyards, on our backs,
we think of nothing
and it's storm patterns.
You describe the twilight
first as a dull breath of death,
and later as a sex tape
involving too many crayons.
I look at you until my head fills
with leftover tea shards. Until
you are cancer free.

POEM EXCLUDING TAXES

On this day in history
the moon died of natural causes.
Astronauts were unavailable
for comment. Though there
was a white silence
in all the rabbit-shaped clouds.
To comfort you, I read a bedtime
story where everything
died of natural causes.
It began: *On this day in history*
the moon died of natural causes,
though we still dreamed it was full.
You shrunk beneath the sheets
with the most German of smiles.

POEM EXCLUDING CORPORATIONS

I clean your clock until you are
Catholic. I occupy everything behind
your eyes or save a seat until you
arrive. When I speak, my breath
moves like a shadow of a cloud over a
field of beardless Amish youth. In the
darkness, my yawn aches. I like to
confess the rarest of dance moves in
total drunkenness.

POEM EXCLUDING COLOR

We sculpt our bodies until
we resemble the town drunk
or the sky after it's moved indoors.
The sky as a carbonated version
of an empty room. Then clouds.
If this were in color, we would
only see red. We would reconsider
our last requests, and let our organs
decay in silence. Become the weather
that repeats and repeats
in another geography.

POEM EXCLUDING ANSWERS

Someone spends her entire life
dreaming of how it will end.
It makes her sad. We sail
a small boat within her heart
and discover another heart,
though it looks more like a moon
lit from within by a single
exploding bottle rocket.

POEM EXCLUDING SHOPPING CARTS

The air moves through the window
like it knows something you don't.
Imagine the first mosquito. Imagine
us baking cakes in the shape of our
future children. They look more like
mountains in a world without people.
Outside the sky grows up. And a
single cloud moves over the backyard
and rain comes down like jeweled
knives in a folk song.

POEM EXCLUDING LANDFILLS

The ground prays at night.
You empty moonlight
over something like the cosmos
of Detroit. Everyone's drunk
on the spring version,
on the rented rooms
in the heart of a thrown away lover.
In the background, shame spreads.
It moves quickly into the valleys
and waterways. Your soul regroups
within a Portuguese sonnet
where rugged teenagers fill
the last existing telephone booth
with stale bubblegum.

POEM EXCLUDING PILATES

You categorize the voices in your head
into hanging files, and later cereal box
characters. You sit by the window
and watch the day become a mountain.
Your eyes, a homeland of loneliness.
Birds thatch the roof. And, you think,
we could be in a Bible story,
if there wasn't all this traffic.

POEM EXCLUDING OPPOSITE DAY

Every thought you have becomes
the future tattoos of sad children
in federally funded afterschool
programs. The river gets a life
and then burns. People wait
in line to give blood, to devour
the future. Bird songs carve
through the air until sunset.
It's always December
in the next chapter of your life,
your thoughts slowly replaced
by freezing rain.

POEM EXCLUDING ONLINE DATING

In the cemetery, we are the Golden Age
of Buzzcuts. The shadows conjugate
the sunlight into an architecture of
loss. Then evening with its interns.
And the perfect mother feeding her
children at a small kitchen table.
And a father grimacing out the window
with a mustache so long it scares small
animals back into the forest. Music peels
the walls in a question of color.

POEM EXCLUDING MATHEMATICS

At the infant's birthday party
we put the cats to sleep
before lighting the trick candles.
You record it all in a journal,
for a script you're working on, you say.
You read the opening sentence
aloud to everyone at the party.
The afternoon is something worth bedazzling.
A security camera pans anxiously
across the parking lot forever.

POEM EXCLUDING MODERN TECHNOLOGY

You fill the pool with cough syrup,
and the hot tub with a thousand
hollowed-out cicada shells.
A man becomes the state bird
in the riflescope of a child,
and the trees remember
themselves as seedlings.
A teenager mistakes his shadow
for an old friend. Together they
think the unthinkable.
You climb a tree
and grow your hair shoulder length.
We are almost too young.

POEM EXCLUDING POLITICS

Everyone we know with brown hair
blonde hair black hair and strawberries
in their mouths on the floor of a silent
house in the suburbs. Everyone we
know with a goatee a mohawk a head
shaved as a symbol of surrender.
Life is what it feels like when you say,
it would be good to see you again.
With shifting weather patterns, and
children constantly gravitating toward
the monkey bars to start another
subculture. The sky moves over them
like a bodyguard in a low budget film.
Everyone we know gives us a look
that says, *I'll tell you later.*

POEM EXCLUDING HAPPY HOUR

The dark feels its way through the
crowd, shows up after the hit & run
on Main Street. Those out of breath
prepare for the credits to run. Those
out of work build a river outside our
window. We watch it move. We grow
headaches throbbing with the spirit
of bad weather, with the Americanism
of extra innings. Spring is a parking
lot filled with dogs in backseats
breathing clouds into the sky.
And the river is a mirror, a mirror
for all the beautiful blondes in the suburbs.
On days like this, the clouds give birth to
other clouds and the rain runs down our
cheeks. On days like this, our
hearts are mistaken for mountains.

POEM EXCLUDING ROMANCE

The first storm seen from outer space
was a ballad. The rest of your life was
summarized in the refrain of a pop
song, in the catching of breath in the
middle of a marathon. We all squint
our eyes at the entire history of
Olympic mascots. As the day grows
into night in bedrooms lit by scented
candles, the obscure noise in the attic
announces how soon the dead
become song.

POEM EXCLUDING SHOWER SCENE

The entire world is room temperature.
Sunlight bleeds over the city,
and the mallwalkers gather
to form a sort of nervous system
or fatigue performance, we say.
Consumers storm the sale racks.
It sounds more and more
like music through pregnant skin.
And today every child is born
into whatever space is available.
We wait for snowfall – maybe
learn another language.
A language built around
the idea of far, far away.

POEM EXCLUDING AGE

We get serious about getting
serious about each other.
Our backyards
want the unblemished version
of night. More stars. More great
lakes, more bodies as rippling
amplifiers. And the first screams
of every next generation will
emerge as floodlights. As
hallucinations under a sky
as dank as a good friend's basement.

POEM EXCLUDING ASTROLOGY

The geese walked in a straight line
across two zip codes. This was your
dream. There was a century's worth of
grief in the surrounding trees, and an
abstract painting trying to capture that
same grief on display at the local
credit union. Something like curtains
came down around us. Like the
hierarchy of pedestrians, everything
was a riddle.

POEM EXCLUDING WITNESSES

As a social experiment you join
a co-ed softball team as a mascot.
Your hairy body in a hairy costume
every Tuesday of summer.
People's faces in the dugout
map the holy places you read
about as a teenager. It's always
the beginning and everything
has changed. During the 5th inning,
you dance your way into the souls
of an entire generation
in the industrial part of town
where the sky loses every time.

POEM EXCLUDING RUST

O, the catchphrases we live.

POEM EXCLUDING CHILDREN

We look at each other until the power
goes out. Until our eyes become sad
hills in an apocalyptic sci-fi thriller.
The sound around us is closer
to the waving of a wet flag
than a fist meeting an enemy's jaw.
In the distance, the lake erases
the last of the windsurfers,
leaving behind only the smell
of clean hair.

POEM EXCLUDING SOPHISTICATION

A season changes in every
conversation we have about
our deceased pets. There's music
and music in the stains of how
we touch each other. And countries
of people in shrunken t-shirts
square dancing the fireflies out
of the black fields they know as *Home*.

POEM EXCLUDING EQUINOX

At first, the sky was a tank top
on a clearance rack, a language
spoken only during funerals
at after-hour clubs with puddles
of sweat on the dance floor.
We say it all with our eyes.
Then hitchhike until everyone
around us has some form of
homemade tattoo. Rain falls
in the periphery. It mimics the
synapses of a pit bull's brain
while chasing a rabbit,
while making love to a sandal.

POEM EXCLUDING MORNING BREATH

For all you know
down the street
the world has ended.
Though the bedroom walls
are still the color
of a foreign disease
we can't pronounce.
I die twice shaving a beard
that gives off a Southern impression.
And it takes everything I have to not
just *bowl* my life away. Any minute
now, earthquakes in the heart
of cupid. There are more times
than not when I need more
than a cupcake is what your eyes
say before we make a baby
you want to name Roza.

POEM EXCLUDING VANDALISM

The hills fill with hip-hop.
And the last tree blooms
through the prologue.
At your wedding,
at your funeral,
we say the same thing
over and over forever.
All the honest children
later become strangers.
The locals drink
until they are invisible.
As if by habit, sadness arrives.
We torture it with a downpour
of faith, with kissing noises.
Later, we don't know how to
look each other in the eyes.

POEM EXCLUDING CITY

The sky was a concussion of clouds
and notorious for dropping everything
at a moment's notice. And the fog,
how it removed everything and then it didn't.
People gathered in the distance and made history
until it hurt. They devoured field after field
with bad ideas and took pride in the
groomed ruins. It was never a photo
opportunity. The mood when the forest
met the asphalt: *Too little, too late.*

POEM EXCLUDING DIALOGUE

We put on all the clothes we own
when the weatherman says, *snow*.
You say all weathermen are the same.
All snowflakes different.
In Hollywood,
they produce the film version
of us walking down the winter street.
It begins with
the camera panning
through every pearl
of snow. We enter
the frame as a blur
amongst the pine trees
in a radiant slo-mo.
You say things
in the slushy street
that will later become a novella.
At the movie première,
all your lines have been cut
and I don't have a mouth.

POEM EXCLUDING NATURE

In my finest pair of blue jeans,
I win the lottery.
You give me everyone
else's face on your deathbed.
No news is good news, you say.
But you want to say more.
You want to say things
that bring to mind a cold rain.
I check my watch, my piggy bank,
and the weather channel
before responding.

POEM EXCLUDING AIR QUOTES

Start with how your father died.
In the hospital, his legs
couldn't even whisper beneath
the thin sheets. You sat in a plastic
chair and took in a view of the parking
garage. The hallway was busy
with the occasional sound of toddlers
chasing balloons, of nurses, fake smiles.
You decorated his bedside with a get-
well card from an ex-wife, a tall glass
of ice water. When he passed, you
wondered how many people
had died in this room,
on this bed,
at this time of night
when the darkness was making
a meal of the world.

POEM EXCLUDING MECHANICS

Beyond City Hall the sun flattens
into a sort of messy bruise
over the lake. A fisherman drinks
until he sees his dead brother
in a dark wave. The sky at the edge
of the suburbs becomes nothing
more than a sad character in a
children's story. Poets gather
at the piano bar for a group photo.
It feels like the end of the imagination.

POEM EXCLUDING GUN CONTROL

Every morning begins with
the saddest story ever told.
The neighborhood kids
pull triggers between
gasps of laughter.
Birds fall from the sky
one at a time. And we wake
to someone's conclusion,
to a rhapsody,
a trumpet cry of sirens.
As far as tomorrow goes,
it's too far away, but you will be there
in the middle trembling.
We can say that much
tightening our belts,
metal purring against our legs.
We understand this may be
our last day to speak of love,
to choke on pistachios on porches
with old friends or the girl with eyes
so brown they could be countries
scarred with the richest of soil.

POEM EXCLUDING BABYSITTER

As we drive past the cemetery,
we hold our breath for several minutes.
Our faces grow obscene floral patterns.
In our breathlessness, our skulls empty
themselves. Trees in winter. Our children in
the backseat become the moral of the story –
startling us with propaganda, with sudden
musicality, with their small, loose teeth.

POEM EXCLUDING DEATH

"The heart is the most donated
organ," she began her lecture. You
listened intently with your painted
face. You thought of heaven. Thought
of all the possible regions. The region
of common nose bleeds. The region
of detective dialogue. The region of
hospital haircuts. The region of
invisible friends. The region of fancy
candy dishes. The region where
science is understood as fact.

POEM EXCLUDING SOUND

We are only fingers pointing
at the rain. Footprints that lead
to gravestones in a children's story
about sharing. About AIDS.
The dying balloons rendezvous
in the sporting goods section,
as we sit in a café and share our
dreams through innovative
hand gestures. It's a sad sight
to the tourists, but they photograph
it anyway. You flash a smile as if to
say there are museums in all of us.

POEM EXCLUDING SMALL TALK

How isn't the weather?
The parking is more
than a bitch,
a cancerous mole.
The water cooler is filled
with holy water. And we fuck
until she's wearing my chest
hair as a holiday sweater.
Until we see the fifty
states of each other.
The sweater off her back
or the way she remembers
the body of her youth.
The wind fingers the leaves
like hors d'oeuvres of the rich
as we ready ourselves
for whatever we believe
is an afterlife.

POEM EXCLUDING WELFARE

You never took the train,
took yourself seriously.
In the dream, you share
a cigarette with everyone
you've ever met on a fire escape,
on a whale watching charter.
"The ocean has always wanted to
swallow us," you remind your only
son at his funeral. At the end
of every cigarette, there you are
addressing history, anchors of
smoke falling through you.

POEM EXCLUDING GOVERNMENT

We empty an entire can of gold spray paint
onto each other. We want to feel rich.
Shine like birds caught in the afterglow
of fireworks. Something else happens
all the time. So we watch the seasons change.
We cross the bridge barefoot in the rain
until our throats become museums.
Museums of gumball trinkets swelling.
We want to feel clean. To understand
the foundations of sadness beginning
with the needs of children. Children who
pout the beautiful out of every single day.

POEM EXCLUDING HI-FIVE

Every winter the lake prepares
for ice skates. The sky makes
epitaphs from the clouds
and the tooth fairy is in a strip club,
three sheets to the wind. Time descends
over the highway. Children and snowplows
collect near the outskirts. Traffic looms
like hymns in the Bible. Beautiful are
the people careening through the wooded
landscape of your photographic memory.

POEM EXCLUDING RED ROVER

Today we send a crow over, our
thoughts paginated as to show how
the mind goes down hill over the
frenzied course of an afternoon in the
yoked light of spring, summer, winter,
look faraway until we're inside the
weather, inside a hypothesis, the
adjectives of a favorite song, lonely,
lonely buildings in the dark where
someone else is singing.

POEM EXCLUDING BEAUTY PAGEANT

And the look on everyone's face
when you gave birth to the baby,
when you left the country of
who you always thought you were,
and stared out the window drinking
in the unbroken sky. Your inner
thoughts simply river and part,
river and part.

POEM EXCLUDING CHANGE

Today every person in the world
is born again, again. Every single
person in the entire world is wearing
a black t-shirt storming
the nearest shoreline.
Today, summer is slang
for summer, is locked inside
every parked car in the city
and the wind is nothing more
than a collection of brilliant sighs.

POEM EXCLUDING GUYLINER

A man serves our cat
love potion from a Big Gulp.
We watch from the bedroom
window and imagine living
in a smarter Texas.
It was a stormy evening,
and our kisses were filled with
potholes and bagpipes.
After the storm, the clouds
took the long way home
in a story coded with bliss.

POEM EXCLUDING NOSTALGIA

It turns out we've been analyzing life
more than living it. So we draw
pictures of what we would look like
as parents. And later, as grandparents
with nose jobs. Grandparents with
nose jobs in a video game where
the world is a large, flat field cluttered
with squawking flamingos.

POEM EXCLUDING YOU

Our prayers come back
as pets lying by our sides
in the season of being famous.
In the season of absolutely nothing.
Our prayers give us cities
full of strangers
informed by failure.
Informed by a calling
it as it is. Inside these
cities there are scars.
Scars we translate into
ghost stories of
immoral light
that juice out of
all people, places, things.

POEM EXCLUDING ELEGY

We peel potatoes in first class in
the Idaho of your dream. Near the back
of the plane I wave a flag completely
constructed of stars. You wake up in a
yawn of turbulence and watch a river
30,000 feet below snake away like jazz.
We are flying over the heartland, and
the sky waits for God. The rich folks
in first class with warm cookies wait
for God. Out swell the clouds of
interpretation, and we become
children in their presence. Point at
that one and that one. Below the
roads go on without us. Like veins
they swell and disappear into fields
meant for no one at all.

POEM EXCLUDING THE END

Fields of fields of fields of coffee in the
moonlight. Words roll off the
tongue and into cities powered by
wind and sex. By sexy wind. We'll
make the most of it. Everyone else
will move to New York, and later
move out of New York and tell stories
about their time in New York until
New York becomes just another strip
mall, until New York becomes just
another Oh.

ACKNOWLEDGMENTS

I am grateful to the editors of the following publications where some of these poems firstappeared, sometimes in altered form:

The Awl, Brooklyn Rail, Columbia Poetry Review, Conduit, Colorado Review, Crazyhorse, Denver Quarterly, Diagram, Forklift, Ohio, Handsome Journal, Hardly Doughnuts, Harvard Review, The Literary Review, Paper Darts, Pinwheel Journal, Ploughshares, Salt Hill Journal, South Dakota Review, Washington Square Review, and *Winter Tangerine Review.*

"Poem Excluding Fiction" appeared in Poets.org and the anthology *Poem-a-Day: 365 Poems for Every Occasion,* Abrams Books 2015

*

Huge thanks to Kristina Marie Darling, David Rossitter, and the entire staff at Tupelo Press for their vision, support, and care.

Love and thanks to Michael McGriff for his brilliant insight and attention to these poems. Equal love and thanks to the friends and family who have supported me in the making of this book, including, in particular, Richie Hofmann, Marcus Jackson, Zach Savich, Natalie Shapero, Tyler Meier, David Hall, Andrew Grace, Tory Weber, Kevin Cain, Graham Foust, Ben Jura, Kyle Marler, "Swannie" Jim Watkins, Rick Smith, Robert Sturm, Joe Hall, Rachelle Toarmino, Brian Pawloski, Gregg Gallson, Mathias Svalina, Matt McBride, Al Abonado, Joshua Ware, Jason Rothschild, Joel Brenden, Theresa & Robert Wierzba, Brian Gerhardstein, Chris Shea, Mike Ostendorf, Phil Brockman, and Stephen "T" Payne.

Many thanks and shout-out-louds to the following institutions and the fine people who work to support poetry, art, and joy: Just Buffalo Literary Center, Kenyon Review Young Writers Workshop, TNH, & Silo City.

Jane, Russ, & Zach Falck for the constant push.

And lastly thanks most deeply to you, reader.

Noah Falck is the author of *Snowmen Losing Weight* (BatCat Press, 2012), *You Are In Nearly Every Future* (Dostoyevsky Wannabe, 2017), and the co-editor of *My Next Heart: New Buffalo Poetry* (BlazeVOX Books, 2017). He lives in Buffalo, New York, where he works as Education Director at Just Buffalo Literary Center and curates the Silo City Reading Series, a multimedia poetry series inside a 130-foot abandoned grain elevator.

MARCUS JACKSON

CPSIA information can be obtained
at www.ICGtesting.com
Printed in the USA
FSHW012204140920